*Submission To God…
God's Strategy*

Submission To God…
God's Strategy

P. Mary Whitehurst

Copyright © 2011 by P. Mary Whitehurst.

ISBN: Softcover   978-1-4568-5807-0

All rights reserved. No part of this book may be reproduced or transmitted in any form or by any means, electronic or mechanical, including photocopying, recording, or by any information storage and retrieval system, without permission in writing from the copyright owner.

This book was printed in the United States of America.

To order additional copies of this book, contact:
Xlibris Corporation
1-888-795-4274
www.Xlibris.com
Orders@Xlibris.com

Contents

Reference Scriptures: 9
Reference Notes 11

God Calls A Divine Reversal 17
Submission to God Pays $$$$$$$$$$$ 19
Trapped By Ignorance 21
Leadership 23
The Godly Home 27
A Family Affair 31
Godly Leadership 33
Submit To Others 35
In the Wilderness 39
To Finish Strong 41
Peace, Sweet Peace 43

About the Author 45

This book is dedicated to my hard working and spiritually gifted family; the Whitehurst—Dawsey, heirs.

I dedicate this theme as a grounding rod; to my daughter, Candace and my grandchildren, Caynebrone, Braylen and Cherish.

Love to Live!!!

Strategy—science or art of war; the planning and directing of military movements and operations; the skillful planning and management of anything plan based on strategy overall plans of a nation at war

Submission—a yielding to the power, control, or authority of another; submitting obedience; humbleness a referring or a being referred to the consideration or judgment of some person or group

Definitions are taken from:

Advanced Dictionary
Scott, Foresman
The Thorndike-Barnhart Series
Copyright 1988, 1983, 1979, 1974, 1973
Scott, Foresman and Company, Glenview, Illinois

Reference Scriptures:

I Tim 2:11

I Tim 3:4

Gen 16:9

Psa 18:44

Psa 66:3

Psa 68:30

Num 10:3

I Cor 16:16

Eph 5:21, 22

Col 3:18

Heb 13:17

Jas 4:7

I Pet 2:13

I Pet 3:1; 5:5

Reference Notes

One In Love

Pg 927 Submission. The New Testament emphasize a voluntary (James 4:7) rather than a forced (Luke 10:17) Submission is appropriate in social roles (as citizen or slave, see Romans 13:1; Titus 2:9. It is also appropriate in Christian interpersonal relationships. Here the image is one of responsiveness and willing to yield to one another out of love.

Pg 930 Mutual Submission. Whenever we move into this area of authority, we tend to emphasize the "right" of the superior to control or influence the person below. Paul immediately showed that control is not the frame of reference from which to begin. His discussion began with the command, "submit to one another out of reverence for Christ"

(Eph. 5:21). We are to maintain a humbleness that considers others—Whatever their place in life was "better than yourselves. Each of you should look not only to your own interests, but also to the interests of others" (Phil 2:3-4) maintaining an attitude of loving concern for one another strips authority of its "rights" and also strips submission of its humiliation. Whatever role we have been given provides an opportunity to serve our brothers and sisters in the Lord.

Occasion to serve. The underlying thought is that authority and submission are not to be viewed as humiliation, but as providing different opportunities to serve.

The Christian attitude toward authority and submission is drastically opposed to the perceptions of the world, which see the one in authority as exalted, and the other as debased. There, each person's value is determined by the position he holds.

But in Christ's church that whole pattern is rejected. Each person's value exists apart from his role. The Christian view of authority and submission shifts the focus completely from power, to service.

Pg 1026 The Call To Submission

Submission. The Greek term are hypotaso or hypotage. The words indicate a subjection or subordination. While this may be forced (as the demons who submit to God (Luke 10:17), Christian submission is voluntary. We submit to secular authority (Rom 13:1), to one another (Eph. 5:21), and Christian slaves even choose submission to harsh masters (I Peter 2:18). Here Peter called on us to submit when persecuted, and keep on trusting God.

Submission's Path—I Pet 2:13—3:9

Plan Authority—I Pet 2:13-17

We Christians submit to authorities "instituted among men" (v.13) for the Lord's sake. Doing good is always within the framework of our society.

Unjust Authorities—I Pet 2:18-25

What if people in authority treat us unjustly? The Christian's call to a life of submission is not conditional. Another person's failure to live God's way does not release us from our responsibility to so submit. To show us that God does not ask of us anymore than He was

Himself willing to do, Peter invites us to look at Jesus. Christ suffered, for doing only good! Even though He might have, Jesus did not retaliate. In His submission Jesus gives us an example of how we are to live.

Husbands and Wives—I Pet 3:1-7

In the husband/wife relationship, submission is again enjoined. Here Peter was addressing a problem that exists today, when Christian wives are married to men who "do not believe the word" (v. 1). Peter did not suggest aggressive evangelism. Instead, the wife is to adopt a course of aggressive submission. Quietly demonstrating the inner beauty Jesus brings, wives are to communicate the Lord through the Holy way of submission. Of course, believing husbands are to be considerate (v.7). But, as the slave is not released from the holy way if he has a harsh master, neither is the wife with an inconsiderate spouse.

Pg 1027 Attitude Toward Suffering For Good—I Pet 3:8-12

In it all, our goal is to "live in harmony with one another" (v. 8)

So Peter's concern is that unjust treatment never tempt us to return evil for evil; and forsake our commitment to good.

Rom 13:1 "Everyone must submit himself to the governing authorities", Paul said. Because human government is stipulated by God for a good purpose, one who rebels against this authority is rebelling against what God has created.

Pg 1030 When we do right and suffer for it, we can be sure that God intends to use our experience for good. Whatever happens to members of God's family, we can be sure that our loving Father is at work for good.

And we are to live this new life now. Freed by Jesus from bondage to "evil human desires."

We are to live our new lives by "the will of God" (I Pet 4:2)

As Peter explained it, submission is not compromise. It is an expression of the Christian's confidence that Jesus is Lord. It is also an expression of our commitment to live by God's will, rather than by the drives and passions of a lost humanity.

Pg 1031 God's will may lead us into experiences of injustice. It did for Jesus. Yet, in Jesus' submission we find not only an example but also hope. Jesus death and resurrection— accomplishing our salvation— made it plain that God worked His good through His Son's suffering, and He can work good through the suffering of His other children as well.

By committing ourselves to God when we suffer injustice, we let Him work in and through our lives. And so, submission is an aspect of holiness. Yes, holiness is love, and holiness is goodness. But holiness is also submission to the will of God when that will leads to the suffering of injustice. Love, goodness, and submission each demonstrate the fact, that we are separated to God.

Pg 863 Psa 18:44 As soon as they hear of me, they shall obey me: the strangers shall submit themselves unto me.

David looks forward with a believing hope that God would still do him good. He promises himself his enemies should be completely subdued, and that his government should be extensive, so that even a people whom he had not known should serve him.

Reference Notes from The Teacher's Commentary/Lawrence O. Richards, 1987, by Scripture Press Publications, Inc.

God Calls
A Divine Reversal

Your past failures do not disqualify you for God's promise. David gained the heart of God. David spoke prophetically to himself that his enemies would be subdued and that his territory would be enlarged; so much so that those that had never known him would submit to his authority.

Submission to God Pays
$$$$$$$$$$$$

Psa 68:30 Rebuke the company of spearmen, the multitude of the bulls, with the calves of the people, til every one submit himself with pieces of silver: scatter thou the people that delight in war. David had himself been a man of war, but could appeal to God that he never delighted in war and bloodshed for its own sake. (the company of spearmen) They are furious and outrageous as a multitude of bull, fat and wanton as the calves of the people . . . til everyone submit himself with pieces of silver . . .

God will cause those that pose a threat to the cause of Christ in you; to finance your dream. When you change your mind about God; he will remit monies for your submission.

Rom 10:3 For they being ignorant of God's righteousness, and going about to establish their own righteousness have not submitted themselves unto the righteousness of God.

Pg 1982 They were ignorant of God's way of justification, which He has now appointed and revealed by Jesus Christ. They thought they needed not to be beholden to the merit of Christ, and therefore depended upon their own performances as sufficient to make up a righteousness wherein to appear before God, and had a proud conceit in this. Unbelief is non-submission to the righteousness of God.

Taken from:
Teacher's Commentary (pages 863–2088)

Trapped By Ignorance

What you don't know can hurt you. Bring your ignorance to God; ask him and he will direct your path. If you don't submit to God; you will bow to Satan. Don't ignore God. Seek him! He will clothe you with His Righteousness.

I Cor 16:15, 16

v15 I beseech you, brethren, (ye know the house of Stephanas, that it is the firstfruits of Achaia, and that they have addicted themselves to the ministry of the saints,)

v16 That ye submit yourselves unto such, and to everyone that helpeth with us, and laboureth.

The household of Stephanas were the first converts in the region of Greece. They had moreover addicted themselves to the ministry of the Saints to serve the Saints. It is an honor to persons of the hightest rank to devote themselves to the service of the Saints. I do not mean to change ranks and become proper servants to the inferiors, but freely and voluntarily to help them and do good to them in all their concerns.

Leadership

Leaders should have a love addiction to serve the Saints, and the followship. Submit under this order. A labour of love . . . what you make happen for others God will make happen for you.

Eph 5:21—25

v 21 Submitting yourselves one to another in the fear of God.

V 22 Wives, submit yourselves unto your own husbands, as unto the Lord.

v 23 For the husband is the head of the wife, even as Christ is the head of the Church: and he is the Savior of the Body.

v24 Therefore as the Church is subject unto Christ, so let the wives be to their own husbands in everything.

v25 Husbands, love your wives, even as Christ also loved the Church, and gave himself for it;

Pg 2087-2088 There is mutual submission that Christians owe one to another . . .

We must be of a yielding and submissive spirit, ready to do all the duties of the respective places and stations that God has allotted to us in the world.

Wives, submit: The duty prescribed to wives is submission to their husbands in the Lord.

This submission includes the honoring and obeying of them, and that from a principle of love to them.

Husband . . . . Head of the wife: The metaphor is taken from the head in the natural, body, being the seat of reason, of wisdom, and of knowledge, and the fountain of sense and motion.

Christ . . . . Head of the Church: There is a resemblance of Christ's authority over the Church in that headship which God has appointed to the husband. Christ's authority is exercised over the Church for the saving of her from evil and the supplying of her with everything good for her. In life manner should the husband be employed for the protection and comfort of his spouse.

Church is subject unto Christ: With cheerfulness, fidelity, and humility.

Husbands, love your wives: For without this, they would abuse their headship. The love of Christ for His Church is proposed as the example to follow. His love is sincere, pure ardent, and constant, despite the imperfections and failures that she is guilty of. The greatness of His love to the Church appeared in His giving Himself unto death for it.

As the Church's subjection to Christ is proposed as an example to wives, so the love of Christ to His Church is proposed as a pattern to husbands, and while such exemplars are offered to both, and so much is required of each, neither has reason to complain of the divine injunctions.

The Godly Home

What's LOVE got to do with it; EVERYTHING, EVERYTHING, EVERYTHING . . .

Submission to God starts with LOVE and end with LOVE.

Christ is the Head of the Church. The Church is subject to Christ. The greatness of His love to the Church is demonstrated in his giving Himself unto death for it.

The love of Christ (bridegroom) to his Church (bride) is proposed as a pattern to husbands, towards their wives.

God's strategy is to bring man to wholeness.

Colossians 3: 17-24

v 17 And whatever you do in word or deed, do all in the name of the Lord Jesus, giving thanks to God the Father through Him.

v18 Wives, submit to your own husbands as is fitting in the Lord.

v19 Husbands, love your wivves and do not be bitter toward them.

v20 Children, obey your parents in all things, for this is well pleasing to the Lord.

v21 Fathers, do not provoke your children, lest they become discouraed.

v22 Servants, obey in all things your masters according to the flesh, not with eyeservice, as men-pleasers, but in sincerity of heart, fearing God.

v23 And whatever you do, do it heartily, as to the Lord and not to men, v24 knowing that from the Lord you will receive the reward of the inheritance; for you serve the Lord Christ.

A Family Affair

It's a family affair . . . . Love. God's order is divine; it is Heaven on Earth.

God is Pro-Family.

Each family member has a role to play to fulfill order in the home. Submission is the Key . . . Come under the Mission of Christ.

"It's not all about me."

Heb 13:17

Obey those who rule over you, and be submissive, for they watch out for your souls, as those who must give account. Let them do so with joy and not with grief for that would be unprofitable for you.

Godly Leadership

Only be ever yielded. Obey means to submit without reservation. Obedience is the action of submission. With the act of obedience; as a down payment, ask what you will.

Every person must come under authority whether godly or ungodly. Align yourself with godly leadership to the saving of your soul.

James 4:7

Therefore submit to God. Resist the devil and he will flee from you.

O.K. God, It's Your Round

Render your submission to God.

Our whole responsibility as dear children is to submit to our loving Father. If we believe God can protect us, then let him do it. Let go and let God!!!

I Pet 2:13-17

v13 Therefore submit yourselves to every ordinance of man for the Lord's sake, whether to the king as supreme,

v14 or to governors, as to those who are sent by him for th punishment of evildoers and for the praise of those who do good.

v15 For this is the will of God, that by doing good you may put to silence the ignorance of foolish men

v16 as free, yet not using your liberty as a cloak for vice, but as servants of God.

v17 Honor all people. Love the brotherhood. Fear God. Honor the king.

Submit To Others

Your submission to others will silence the mouths of foolish—men.

When you submit to others, you will gain respect in high places.

Remember that you are submitting your cause "for the Lord's sake."

I will commit (in other words; come to it) with my submission to the laws of the land and to it's governing body. It is the will of God and a duty for those that swore to uphold the ordinance of man. Our God is the God of Order. A man of Authority; submits to another's authority.

A person would do well in this; and silence the unreasonable reproaches of the ignorant and foolish men.

I am born to be free; but not to use my freedom as a tool of Satan's wickedness.

Honor all men as created by God the Father. A special affection should be shown for the household of FAITH.

Servants ought to conduct themselves to their masters with submission; for Christ sake.

This is acceptable to God. Christ Jesus is our example. Follow his steps of submission.

Jesus commitment was toward God first and then to humanity.

Our healing is in Jesus' submission to others. This is the glory of the cross. He paid with his blood the price for our sin. Jesus bore our sins in his own body on the tree. We were all astray until Jesus stepped in and redeemed our souls. He was totally committed/submitted to humanity.

Wives be true in your submission to your own husband. The husband may not receive the word readily; but he will come back to it. Because the WORD shall not go out void; but it shall accomplish what God said.

The husband is the spiritual covering for his wife. The husband is the bond of safety for his home. The wife would do well to have this priestly, anointed vessel; her husband to establish covenant relationships in the home.

Wives, fear (respect) God. Your discipline is priceless. Wives are not to be afraid of your husband; but a healthy respect is pleasing to God.

Husbands live life to the MAXX, as knowing Christ. Hold your wife in high esteem; at all times; recognizing her weak moments. Together, you inherit the grace of God's favor.

For your appreciation; your prayers will not be hindered.

In the Wilderness

Who you are spiritually covered by determines the greatness of your inheritance. God chose Abram for greatness; so everything in his house would experience the exceedingly great blessing.

The fact that Hagar was a member of Abram's household; was her call to destiny. She was to reap the benefit of the promise inheritance. The minute you conceive it . . . seems that all HELL break loose. But, Hagar had to experience her wilderness. There was instability in the place she called home. She chose to run away from her spiritual covering (authority). The angel called her out by name and position, and told her to return and submit under Sarai's hands (signifying blessing). The angel announced a great increase for her.

In all of your upsets— RUN to God!!!

He is the only one responsible for your set-ups.

The tendency to flee, give up, throw in the towel, quit or otherwise be discouraged comes before the advancement to your next level.

No matter how far you've strayed . . . . You can come back to the RAY OF HIS LIGHT; and meet your assigned position in God.

Cry if you have to; but come on back (repentance). Name your wilderness experience . . . Ishmael, "God will hear."

To Finish Strong

Be all of one mind; having the mind of Christ. To inherit a blessing . . . counter attack evil; with a blessing to another.

Your attitude (mood, thoughts, and action) determines your altitude (high place).

Suffering is a part of the submission process; as we allow God to work in and through our lives.

Finally, you are submitting your call . . . HIS cause; for the Lord's sake.

Peace, Sweet Peace

Job 22:21

Submit to God and be at peace with him . . . thereby good will come to you.

My arms are too short to box with God. My way won't work!

    Get out of Your way (self destruction) and into God's Way.

    He is the WAY . . . WAY MAKER.

    It's a High Way . . . . to the Heavenly Place.

    I surrender ALL!!!

    Total Submission to God . . . I am at Peace.

About the Author

Pastor/Evangelist P. Mary Whitehurst is the founding Pastor/President of Vision Ministries, Inc., Dothan, AL.

Vision Ministries, Inc. is established to administer help to the sick, needy, homeless and poor in spirit.

Vision Ministries, Inc. is Dothan's primer interdenominational outreach ministry.

The outreach ministry's revelatory scripture is Proverbs 29:18... Where there is no VISION, the people perish; but he that keepeth the law, happy is he.

Evangelist Whitehurst heard the call of salvation in 1979 with the gospel message:

> "It's not how long you make it . . . . but how you make it long."

She has served in many capacities within Triumph The Church and KOGIC; the church from her birth. Through her faithfulness, God entrusted her with Vision Ministries, Inc., in 1991. Pastor Whitehurst has been a church and community leader for over 25 years.

This book entitled, Submission To God . . . God's Strategy is a reflection from the message (Submission To God) ministered by Pastor Carlton Pearson at Higher Dimensions Evangelistic Center in 1991.

Over the course of my spiritual journey; I can see how God uses strategies to perfect his purpose and plan for my life.

CPSIA information can be obtained at www.ICGtesting.com
Printed in the USA
LVOW080141020413

327061LV00001B/88/P